Scotla

Railways

The Last 15 Years

STUART FOWLER

BRITAIN'S RAILWAYS SERIES, VOLUME 9

Rear cover image: Class 56s made a welcome return to Scotland, following the initial withdrawal of the type by EWS in 2004, when Colas Rail brought a number back into service. On 23 May 2018, 56094 is seen at Gailles, between Irvine and Barassie, while working 6R46, the loaded 06.30 Grangemouth to Prestwick Airport aviation fuel tanks.

Contents page image: Black 5 45407 makes light work as it crests the summit at Plean on 21 August 2011 while working 1Z29, the 09.52 Linlithgow to Dalmeny SRPS railtour.

Published by Key Books
An imprint of Key Publishing Ltd
PO Box 100
Stamford
Lincs PE19 1XQ

www.keypublishing.com

The right of Stuart Fowler to be identified as the author of this book has been asserted in accordance with the Copyright, Designs and Patents Act 1988 Sections 77 and 78.

Copyright © Stuart Fowler, 2020

ISBN 978 1 913870 25 6

Typeset by SJmagic DESIGN SERVICES, India.

Contents

Introduction

For most of my life, I have been around railways. I started out, like many youngsters in the hobby, by collecting locomotive numbers and getting that sense of achievement from seeing the last one that I needed of a particular class. Over the years, my interest in that gave way as I pursued photography with an aim of trying to record the developing railway scene, primarily in Scotland and northern England along with other areas of the UK, as time permitted.

I have decided to compile this book by presenting the variety and the changes that have occurred within Scotland during the past 15 years on a regional basis, namely the south west, south east, central, north east and the Highlands. To give as much balance as possible to each section, the regions have been somewhat stretched, the details of which can be found in the individual chapters.

The last 15 years have seen a huge amount of change in the rail network within Scotland, from the replacement of old rolling stock with new trains, an explosion of colourful liveries, the re-opening of routes, the demise of coal trains and the boom of container freight traffic. Yesterday is most definitely history and this book, through about 190 photos, looks to review this variety, ranging from the everyday to the unusual that has and can be seen. While it would be ideal to include everything, I have focused on what I consider to be worthy of publication, including a few oddities and rarities.

Looking at passenger operations, new routes have opened during the period of focus, including those to Larkhall and Alloa along with the Airdrie to Bathgate extension and the Borders route to Tweedbank. Furthermore, electrification has changed a number of the lines beyond recognition with overhead wires now on the Edinburgh to Glasgow routes via both Falkirk and Shotts, along with the suburban route out of Glasgow to Paisley Canal. Of course, these changes have brought about a shift in traction with new electric units ousting the diesels. Likewise, the introduction of HSTs on services between the Scottish cities has brought much interest back to the passenger scene.

In contrast, the freight market has unfortunately been in decline for some time, compounded significantly by the loss of coal traffic, which accounted for a substantial volume. It is not all doom and gloom, however, as container traffic has continued to increase while there are plenty of other workings across the main routes. In addition, new freight operating companies have appeared, bringing much heritage traction back to the scene. This book will look at the variety of traffic and the locos that power these freight trains across the country.

I have to caveat from the outset that as a photographer living in the south west of Scotland, there is perhaps a slightly biased feel to the book in that I have been able to record local movements in much greater detail than other areas. This book will take us on a tour of Scotland and, while the west and central areas feature slightly more prominently, the other regions have not been neglected. I have aimed to keep the variety as wide as possible and I hope you enjoy the selections that I have made.

For enthusiasts, Scotland can be a difficult place to photograph with poor weather a constant source of frustration, not to mention the low frequency of trains on certain routes at times. While these are downsides, Scotland has much to offer in terms of scenery. Additionally, there are still semaphore signals on a number of routes and the liveries of the trains are plentiful. Of course, rolling stock is varied too depending on where you go. To emphasise this point, no fewer than 45 different class of trains are featured in this book.

I am aware that a lot of people are curious about the equipment we use as photographers so I will give a little bit of background to what I use, and have used. I began photography with a manual Centon SLR body with a fixed 50mm lens along with a 70-210mm zoom. While this was good at the time, its limitations became obvious when manual focusing took a bit of thought and time, which is not always possible when you arrive at a location just as the train is approaching!

As my career as a quantity surveyor was developing and disposable income was not an issue, I soon purchased a Canon EOS 1000, which believe it or not is still in use today. I have used various lenses including a 50mm fixed, 135mm fixed, 28-90mm and a 70-300mm, all auto-focus. I am probably a bit of a dinosaur when it comes to photography as I still use colour slide film when we have 'full sun' days, although these are rare in Scotland! I enjoy using this medium and feel it keeps me on my toes; however, this is all down to personal preference and this is what I enjoy using. I was probably a late starter to digital, buying my first Canon EOS body in 2012. The images used throughout this book are a mixture of both colour slides and digital.

Like many who have written books before, this has only been possible with the support of good friends, contacts within the industry, my mum and Fiona, thank you all. Without this support, many of the photos recorded in this book would simply not be possible. I am dedicating this book to the memory of my sister, Arlene Fowler.

Freightliner 86610 leads sister 86628 south at Wandel Mill, north of Abington, on the 24 March 2018 while working south with the Saturday-only 4M83 10.31 Coatbridge to Crewe Bashford Hall.

Chapter 1

The South East

This chapter extends to cover the East Coast Main Line (ECML) from Berwick to Edinburgh and out to Auchengray on the line heading towards Carstairs, along with the Borders link to Tweedbank.

The south east has seen some considerable changes in the past 15 years along with a fascinating variety of traction. In the past year, the ECML has seen the decline of the Class 91 loco-hauled trains, which have worked this route since their introduction, these being ousted by the new Azuma units. The Hitachi-built fleet also contains a number of bi-mode trains, which allows them to run through services to both Inverness and Aberdeen. This in turn has allowed LNER to hand back the ageing HST fleet.

The Class 91s have carried a variety of liveries in the period that I am covering, ranging from GNER blue to East Coast silver and Virgin/LNER red/white. A number of the fleet have also received one-off special vinyls, these including 91101 with *Flying Scotsman* brandings, 91110 with Battle of Britain Memorial Flight colours, 91111 in a commemorative World War One livery and named *For the Fallen* and, of course, 91119, which was repainted back into InterCity colours. I have included a number of these locos, which have proven to be of much interest to railway photographers. Of course, the HSTs on the east coast route have also carried a number of the above liveries, although, apart from the blue/grey set, the most unique power cars have been those with individual motifs such as 'Craigentinny 40' to celebrate the anniversary of the depot in Edinburgh.

Rolling stock used on the commuter traffic between Edinburgh and North Berwick has been interesting to say the least. Following the withdrawal of the ageing Class 305 fleet, the line has seen the use of Class 322 EMUs, which were brought north from England and worked in two different periods, along with Class 318s, Class 380s and, most recently, Class 385s. During the first half of 2005, the services were in the hands of ex-Virgin Mk3 coaches and DVTs with Class 90s being provided by EWS. These locos offered an eclectic mix of liveries including Railfreight Distribution, GNER and EWS examples. Their use was brought about due to a lack of available stock on the network.

Freight traffic on the east coast has suffered, like many other areas of Scotland, due to the decline in coal movements with the loading point at Blindwells unfortunately closing by 2005. However, Cockenzie Power Station was still receiving coal from a variety of locations, including Hunterston on the west coast of Scotland. Both Freightliner and EWS/DB were working these trains at the time and, for a while, coal trains were also being loaded at Leith Docks.

Away from coal traffic, a regular and long-lived freight that has since ceased running was the daily 'binliner' from Powderhall to Oxwellmains, near Dunbar. This containerised refuse train could employ a variety of traction including Classes 37, 60, 66 or 67. A number of other freight trains pass through this area, including the steel trains to Dalzell at Motherwell, the Alcan tanks from Blyth to Fort William and the intermittent pipe train from Hartlepool to Georgemas, where the pipes are collected for use by the North Sea oil industry. Recently, container traffic has returned with a flow between Mossend and Tees Dock. The South East also witnesses regular nuclear traffic to Torness Power Station operated by DRS.

This brings us on to the construction of the Borders Railway, which began in 2012 and was opened in 2015. There had been a long-standing pressure on the Scottish Government to reinstate the line to Tweedbank owing to the growing communities in the borders region and to reduce the volume of traffic into Edinburgh at peak times. On 9 September 2015, the official opening train with HM The Queen on board ran with A4 60009 *Union of South Africa*; the weather that day was of course dull and cloudy! The line sees steady commuter traffic worked by Class 158s and 170s, but it has also proven popular with railtours since it re-opened, bringing the use of both steam and diesels. It will be interesting to see what happens in the future as the extension to Carlisle has been spoken about; through trains on the Waverly Route could well return once again!

I have also included in this section the line running towards Carstairs as far as Auchengray. This has allowed me to include a photo of the Caledonian Sleeper running behind a Freightliner Class 90, which were hired in for a while due to availability issues with GB Railfreight Class 92s.

The coastal section of the East Coast Main Line features in this view of DVT 82204 as it heads south near Lamberton on 9 August 2014 while leading 1E16, the 13.00 Edinburgh Waverly to London King's Cross.

This is the only photograph I have of a pair of Class 91s. On 20 March 2020, 91102 *City of York* and 91124 top 1S04, the 06.15 King's Cross to Edinburgh Waverly, at Houndwood.

The Hitachi-built LNER Azuma units have made quite an impact on services between Edinburgh and London, ousting the Class 91s. Both all electric and bi-mode sets are in service. On 20 March 2020, 801213 looks purposeful while working south with 1E12, the 11.00 for King's Cross from Edinburgh, at Houndwood.

The loops at Grantshouse, south of Dunbar, offer freights a chance to make way for the regular class one passenger traffic. On 20 March 2020, 66084 has been pulled into the loops while working the late running 4E99 08.24 Mossend to Tees Dock intermodal, a train which has proven to be very successful. Note the loco has lost its EWS branding in lieu of DB stickers, although it retains its first owner's livery.

Flying Scotsman-branded 91101 powers north past East Fortune on 30 November 2019 with 1S08, the 08.30 King's Cross to Edinburgh Waverly.

The most recent EMU type to work the North Berwick services are the Class 385s. On 9 April 2019, 385005 leads the 12.28 from North Berwick to Edinburgh Waverly on the approach to Drem Junction, where it joins the East Coast Main Line.

A train that unfortunately no longer runs is the Edinburgh 'binliner' from Powderhall to Oxwellmains. The timings of the train offered a number of good photo opportunities. In this case, 67004 heads north near Drem Junction with 6B46, the 12.43 Oxwellmains to Powderhall, on 5 November 2014.

In a great gesture by LNER, 91119 *Bounds Green InterCity Depot 1977-2017* received a repaint back into InterCity Swallow colours to celebrate the use of the locos on the ECML as their demise continues. Looking smart on 25 July 2019, the AC electric heads north past Drem loops with 1S10, the 09.30 King's Cross to Edinburgh Waverly.

During an absolute deluge of rain, Railfreight triple grey 60063 *James Murray*, with an EWS 'Beastie' sticker on the bodyside, passes through Drem on 3 September 2008 with 6B45, the 10.25 Powderhall to Oxwellmains 'binliner'.

Carrying a white stripe instead of red following the takeover of the East Coast franchise by National Express from GNER, DVT 82220 flies south at Drem with 1E10, the 10.00 Edinburgh Waverly to King's Cross service, on 8 September 2010.

The distinctive yellow pipes give this train away as being the sporadic 6X88 05.38 Hartlepool to Georgemas Junction. The train is seen behind 66100 *Armistice 100 1918-2018* on 9 April 2019 between Drem and Longniddry. It is common practice for the train to recess at Mossend until the early evening prior to heading north onto the Highland Main Line.

ScotRail operates fast services between Edinburgh and Dunbar using Class 385s but, for a while, Class 380s were used. On a bright 17 February 2018, 380111 charges along towards Longniddry at Redhouse Castle with the 11.02 Dunbar to Edinburgh.

This 27 June 2007 image shows 322481 arriving into Longniddry with the 11.17 from North Berwick to Edinburgh Waverly.

The coal workings between Millerhill and Cockenzie Power Station offered plenty of trains during the day to photograph. For a short while, coal was being moved by Freightliner from Ravenstruther to Cockenzie. 66564 is about to set back to the unloading terminal on 3 April 2009, having arrived with the 6B36 11.15 working from Ravenstruther.

Having also lost its red GNER stripe, 91127 races towards Prestonpans on 3 April 2009 with 1S11, the 10.00 London King's Cross to Edinburgh Waverly.

'Celebrity' 91111 *For the Fallen* approaches Prestonpans on 17 February 2018 with 1S13, the 11.00 departure from London to Edinburgh.

A complete National Express East Coast-liveried HST heads south at Prestonpans on 26 May 2012 with 43320 leading 1E13, the 07.55 Inverness to King's Cross.

This image shows the transition from National Express to East Coast underway with 43309 heading 1E11, the 07.52 Aberdeen to London, on the approach to Prestonpans on 26 May 2012.

The Virgin East Coast livery suited the HSTs well. By now operating with LNER, 43206 races towards Wallyford with the 07.52 Aberdeen to King's Cross (1E11) once again on 25 July 2019.

GNER blue 43112 heads out of Edinburgh at Musselburgh on 23 November 2007 with 1E13, the 07.55 Inverness to King's Cross.

With its GNER red stripe replaced with a white band, 43314 rolls into Edinburgh Waverly with a morning service from London to Aberdeen on 3 September 2008.

Due to a shortage of stock, ScotRail hired a number of Class 158s to provide assistance to its fleet. In a bizarre twist, two of these units arrived from South West Trains. On 27 June 2007, 158786 awaits departure time at Edinburgh Waverly with the 14.11 service for Newcraighall.

National Express-liveried 158709 runs into Haymarket on 28 June 2007 with a morning Dunblane to Edinburgh service.

158868 meanders towards Stow on 9 April 2016 with a morning service from Edinburgh Waverly to Tweedbank.

Since its re-opening, the Borders line has seen a number of railtours operated by a variety of locos. D9009 *Alycidon* powers towards Stow loops on 9 April 2016 with 1Z54, the 04.55 Derby to Tweedbank.

On 15 May 2016, 60103 *Flying Scotsman* worked a tour from Edinburgh to Tweedbank. Union Flag-branded 47580 *County of Essex* was on the rear of the train and is seen shortly before departing back north with 1Z23, the 15.56 Tweedbank to Edinburgh. The station at Tweedbank is a minimal affair with two platforms.

The CrossCountry services between Glasgow and Edinburgh via Carstairs receive little attention. To redress this, 220033 is seen on 13 July 2013 working a Glasgow to Bristol service past Harburn.

Due to availability issues with its own Class 92 fleet, GB Railfreight hired in Freightliner Class 90s to assist with operating the Caledonian Sleeper services. At this time, only three locos remained in the original grey livery; therefore, I was very pleased when 90047 rounded the curve at Auchengray on 1 June 2018 with 5B26, the 08.30 Edinburgh Waverly to Polmadie empty coaching stock.

Chapter 2
The North East

I mentioned in the introduction that a bit of manipulation would be required to provide a proportional level of interest between the regions that this book is covering. While the north east is generally focused north of Dundee, this section is going to be pulled back a little further south to capture the Kingdom of Fife, extending as far as the Firth of Forth at North Queensferry and Dalmeny and running west as far as Kincardine. On the western axis, we will capture traffic between Perth and Dundee while the most north-westerly point will be Inverurie.

My library of images for this part of Scotland is somewhat limited for the simple reason that it is further away from the likes of the West Coast Main Line, which is far busier, and was only readily accessible to me after I started driving. However, over the years I have managed to capture a considerable number of photos, both freight and passenger, and I hope those that have been selected provide a small insight into the fascinating variety of trains that I have managed to photograph; it is of course by no means exhaustive.

Fife has always had a strong association with loco-hauled workings, predominantly running at peak times when passenger numbers have been too large for existing stock to cope with. Both EWS and latterly DB Schenker worked the trains using Class 67s and Mk2 coaches, while I have also featured two later workings, both hauled by Direct Rail Services Class 68s and illustrating a complete set of Transport for Scotland-liveried vehicles. These trains have now ceased with ScotRail having sufficient stock to cope with the demand. Will this be the last time we see traditional coaching stock running over the Forth Bridge? We will need to wait and see!

All other Fife circle workings are generally either Class 158s or Class 170s. The express passenger services to Aberdeen for a long time utilised the latter DMUs, which have proven to be very successful units. During 2018, Abellio revealed that it was planning to use former Great Western HSTs on the key city routes between Glasgow, Inverness, Aberdeen and Edinburgh. For a long time, due to delays with refurbishment of the stock, some weird and wonderful combinations of HST sets could be seen, including a full GWR green formation; not something I visualised photographing east of Aberdeen one morning! Moving further north towards Aberdeen, the Class 158s still retain a strong foothold working the services south to Montrose and those towards Inverness.

One of the most interesting aspects of the region is that semaphore signalling still features predominately with many in ideal locations for photography. I have selected a few images that feature these to provide a little variety.

On the freight front, the lines around Inverkeithing were far busier a number of years ago than they are now with freight traffic. The driver behind this shift was predominantly due to the requirement for coal trains to run as far as Dunfermline Queen Margaret before needing to retrace their steps to Dunfermline Town and before heading down the line towards Longannet as the junction to the branch is south facing. This set-up was ideal for the photographer as you could photograph both empty and loaded trains twice around Dunfermline in the space of an hour or so.

Within the period this book is focusing on, the majority of freights were in the capable hands of the Class 66s, which obliterated the older loco fleets such as the Class 37s and Class 56s that had dominated the coal scene for years. Of course, the volume of coal trains would soon fall off a cliff edge as the re-opening of the Stirling-Alloa-Kincardine line took place, which allowed heavier and longer trains to run to Longannet Power Station. Similarly, this removed the need for any run-round shunts.

Coal in Fife made a revival with the announcement that a new loading point at Earlseat Hall was to open. Due to the nature of the facilities, the trains from Earlseat used MEA box wagons, which brought a little variety to the line. The trains ironically passed Longannet and headed down the west coast of Scotland to Hunterston. The port at Hunterston was responsible for the huge volumes of imported coal that Longannet required. At Hunterston, this coal was blended with the imported coal before being sent all the way back to Longannet for burning.

Cement traffic to and from Aberdeen has provided some colourful variety through Fife with both Freightliner Class 66s and Colas locos working these, the latter employing Class 60s and 70s, although the Brush-built locos are now history following their sale to GBRf. Aviation fuel trains had a presence in the region, working to the military airbase at Leuchars, near St Andrews. Unfortunately, following the downgrading of Leuchars, the train no longer runs, although I did manage to capture it a few times.

Moving north of the River Tay, the loaded cement trains from Oxwellmains provide interest, these running via Stirling due to weight limitations over the Tay Bridge. DRS currently works a daily intermodal service from Grangemouth to Aberdeen, which has featured both Class 66 and 68 locomotives, although the General Motors design is the norm.

EWS-liveried 67004 runs off the Forth Bridge and into Dalmeny with the 17.08 Edinburgh to Edinburgh circular on 8 September 2010.

Colas-operated 60002 climbs up Jamestown Viaduct with the empty 6B32 16.52 Aberdeen to Oxwellmains cement train on 28 June 2018.

LNER HST power car 43302 leads 1E25, the 14.25 Aberdeen to King's Cross, across Jamestown Viaduct on 16 August 2016.

Looking absolutely resplendent with a uniform set of coaches in the Transport for Scotland-mandated ScotRail colours, the morning 2G02 07.46 Glenrothes with Thornton to Edinburgh powers up Jamestown Viaduct with 68007 *Valiant* at the helm on 17 July 2017.

66103 skirts the banks of the Firth of Forth at Culross on 20 October 2005 while working a loaded merry-go-round coal train from Hunterston to Longannet Power Station.

Colas Rail took over the Linkswood aviation fuel train in its final year with both Class 56s and 66s featuring. The shore at Culross features in this shot of 66847 as it heads back to Grangemouth with the 6N72 ex-Linkswood, which will travel over the line through Alloa and Stirling on 21 October 2012.

Northern Belle-liveried 47790 *Galloway Princess* makes for an interesting subject as it heads for Dunfermline at Culross on 25 October 2014 with 1Z38, the 11.11 Glasgow Central to Dunfermline and Edinburgh *Northern Belle*.

66182 approaches Kincardine on 7 June 2013 with the 6G26 Earlseat to Hunterston loaded coal train. It was somewhat ironic that the bulk of this coal would be back at Longannet in a matter of a few days after it was blended with imported coal.

Prior to the opening of the Stirling-Alloa-Kincardine line, coal trains had a circuitous route to run via Dunfermline, including a run-round at Townhill loops. 66051 approaches Dunfermline Queen Margaret station on 3 August 2006 with a set of empties from Longannet to Hunterston.

The Scottish Railway Preservation Society has in recent years run railtours from Linlithgow to Dalmeny via the Fife circle and Alloa using a variety of steam locos. On 28 April 2012, it was the turn of 'Royal Scot' 46115 *Scots Guardsman* to take the honours. The morning train is seen passing Cowdenbeath, running as the 1Z46 09.22 from Linlithgow.

The 2L69 17.20 Edinburgh to Cardenden service did not return to Edinburgh, instead it ran empty coaching stock back to Motherwell. During its booked stop in Inverkeithing loop, 68008 *Avenger* sits with the 5L70 18.24 Cardenden to Motherwell on 26 May 2017. Both 68006 and 68007 were specially vinyled to match the train, but with maintenance cycles and the like, non-matching Class 68s were quite common.

The luxury *Royal Scotsman* was powered by the West Coast Railway Company for some time, a period which saw it hauled by Class 33s, 37s, 47s and 57s. On 18 May 2014, a pair of Class 37s in the shape of 37516 *Loch Laidon* and 37685 *Loch Arkaig* storm towards Dalgety Bay with the 1Z23 13.35 Edinburgh to Ardgay via Perth and Inverness.

A loco that seems to follow me around is 66101. I have images of this on coal, containers, fuel, cement, steel and, as seen here, infrastructure duties. On 18 May 2014, the loco is seen slogging towards Dalgety Bay with a loaded ballast train from Millerhill to Alloa.

In a welcome gesture by LNER, one of its HSTs was painted into retro blue/grey livery and used over a number of routes before the full withdrawal of the fleet. On a sunny and crisp 18 December 2019, 254029 leads the 1Z43 09.46 Edinburgh Waverly to Inverness via Aberdeen out of Cupar with 253003 on the rear.

Wormit, to the south of the Tay Bridge, provides a number of photographic opportunities. In a fortunate burst of sunshine, 43163 powers south with an unrefurbished set of stock on the early lunchtime Dundee to Edinburgh empty coaching stock move on 11 October 2019.

Errol, between Perth and Dundee, still retains some charm with a signal box, 'pegs' and a level crossing. On 29 October 2018, 70812 approaches the box with 6A65, the 05.55 Oxwellmains to Aberdeen cement train.

For the past few years, GB Railfreight has run a charity train for its staff with the donations going to selected causes. One benefit of this is that it has brought unusual locos to certain areas. In gorgeous morning sunshine, the BR blue pair of 20096 and 20107 rattles over the crossing at Errol with the 1Z15 08.15 Edinburgh to Inverness via Aberdeen on 10 September 2016.

In 2018, the new Mk5 sleeper stock began to arrive in the UK for use on the overnight services between Scotland and England to replace the ageing Mk2/3 coaches. For a while, the usual driver training and staff familiarisation took place. On 13 September 2019, 73968 leaves Dundee with a 5Z74 09.40 Aberdeen Clayhills to Polmadie empty coaching stock move.

On the approach to Arbroath, 43012 is seen heading south with an afternoon service from Aberdeen to Glasgow Queen Street on 13 September 2019. This was taken during a time of transition when the majority of HST sets were still running with the ex-First Great Western-liveried coaches.

Wearing its full Inter7City livery, 43136 passes the signal box at Inverkeilor on 8 August 2020 with 1A53, the 08.41 Glasgow Queen Street to Aberdeen.

Bi-mode Azuma 800106 forms the 1E15 09.52 Aberdeen to King's Cross as it heads south near Inverkeilor on 8 August 2020.

The northern approach to Montrose features in this image taken on 15 August 2019 as 170428 approaches the station and passes the signal box and semaphores with a midday departure from Aberdeen to Glasgow Queen Street. Montrose, at the time of writing, is a starting/terminating point for stopping local services from Aberdeen.

158713 approaches Craigo signal box, between Montrose and Laurencekirk, on 26 August 2019 with a Montrose to Aberdeen stopping service.

A longstanding intermodal service that runs in the north east is the daily Grangemouth to Aberdeen run by Direct Rail Services. In lovely warm weather, 66424 approaches Carmont, between Laurencekirk and Stonehaven, on 26 August 2019 with the 4A13 from Grangemouth.

Just dodging the impending downpour, British Transport Police-branded 170407 rolls into Stonehaven on 18 February 2020 with the 09.41 Glasgow Queen Street to Aberdeen service. Stonehaven station features a number of semaphores.

With a lack of freight trains, the line between Aberdeen and Inverness is somewhat neglected by photographers. However, there are some lovely locations to record the passenger trains. On 18 February 2020, a pair of Class 158s head into a downpour with the 10.12 Aberdeen to Inverness service west of Inverurie.

Chapter 3

The Highlands

This section of the book will look at what I am defining as the Highlands. This will extend from Inverness to Perth on the Highland Main Line, along with the West Highland Line from Anniesland north to both Oban and Fort William. As most photographers will agree, these lines have some of the most spectacular scenery in Scotland. In addition, both lines have seen an interesting variety of trains, a small selection of which have been picked from my library with the aim of trying to provide as diverse a variety as possible. Similar to the north east, volume of trains is a common problem while a lot of patience is required and the weather is certainly not guaranteed.

Passenger services between Perth and Inverness are limited to Class 158s or 170s along with HSTs and the new Azuma fleet for LNER. Of course, ScotRail has now received a sufficient quota of its refurbished HST sets, but I did manage to capture a number of the unrefurbished sets that provided a little interest.

The overnight sleeper services between London Euston and Inverness have brought quite a bit of variety in recent years in terms of locos. Class 67s from DB were run of the mill on the standard rake of Mk2/3 coaches and I was fortunate enough to photograph a variety of liveries on this train, including one of the Royal duo, which was a little different. In the past year or so, a shift in traction and stock brought further variety in the shape of Mk5 coaches and Class 73/9s. For a while, the train was worked by a Class 66 and Class 73 combination due to problems with the recently rebuilt electro-diesels. However, over the course of time, the Class 73s have settled down and now generally double-head the train. Few could have ever envisaged photographing the former Southern Region locos on the overnight sleeper through the Highlands!

The West Highland Line (WHL) is a bit simpler as passenger operations are firmly in the hands of Class 156s while the sleeper is booked for a Class 73/9 and Mk5 coaches. While the WHL may not have the same volume of passenger trains, the line generally has more railtours to Oban and Mallaig. The world famous 'Jacobite' steam-hauled trains run between Fort William and Mallaig and cross Glenfinnan Viaduct, the scene of the Harry Potter filming, these being operated by the West Coast Railway Company. The *Royal Scotsman* also runs over these lines which, in recent times, has been worked by GB Railfreight, the company normally deploying its specially liveried Class 66 duo of 66743 and 66746.

I have decided to include preservation within this section by featuring the Strathspey Railway, which runs between Aviemore and Broomhill. The line is ten miles long and has a number of photogenic locations. I have included two photographs, one of the line's home steam locos on a service train while the second features the resident Class 31 on the *Royal Scotsman*, which is booked to run through to Boat of Garten.

Freight traffic is again similar to the north east, being a little sparse. The Highland Main Line is the better of the two in terms of volume and variety, it seeing container and cement trains worked by Direct Rail Services and Colas respectively. The Stobart/Tesco container train is an early morning runner heading north from Mossend to Inverness, which then returns in the early afternoon. The cement train is a bit more sporadic and runs once or twice a week, depending on customer demands. This train also heads north in the morning but returns in the early evening. I have included two photographs of this train, featuring the now historic Class 60s along with the now standard Class 70s.

Over on the West Highland, the only regular freight train is the Alcan alumina tanks from North Blyth to the smelter at Fort William. This train is operated by GBRf and uses a Class 66. In the winter months, the dedicated *Royal Scotsman* locos are common on the working as the *Royal Scotsman* season is limited to the summer months.

The Class 68s have been a welcome addition to the Highland Main Line on the Stobart/Tesco train. On a warm 19 July 2016, 68002 *Intrepid* eases off Culloden Viaduct with 4D47, the 13.07 Inverness to Mossend containers.

On 14 April 2018, 66743 and 66746 double-head the *Royal Scotsman* at Slochd as they work south with the 1H81 08.39 Kyle of Lochalsh to Boat of Garten. See the next image for the unusual traction that worked the train to its destination from Aviemore.

In the most fortunate spot of sunshine, D5862 is seen having arrived at Boat of Garten with the 1H81 08.39 from Kyle of Lochalsh on 14 April 2018, which it hauled from Aviemore. The Class 66s that worked the train from Kyle would be stabled at Aviemore until the following morning when the train worked back with the Class 31 before it headed to Dundee.

In this beautiful scene, the Strathspey's Caledonian 828 loco rounds the curve on the approach to Broomhill with the first train of the day from Aviemore on 14 April 2018.

Colas Rail's 60087 *CLIC Sargent* is seen on the approach to Aviemore with the 6H51 02.48 Oxwellmains to Inverness cement train on 19 July 2016. These locos were the workhorses for Colas prior to the decision by the company to transfer its Class 70s north from southern England and sell the Class 60 fleet.

On 19 July 2016, a most unusual combination was atop the overnight sleeper from London to Inverness. Following the revelation that GBRf intended to re-engineer a number of Class 73s the rebuilt locos eventually appeared on the train but not working it. Due to reliability problems, which resulted in availability issues, the train for a while was worked with a Class 66 double-heading the Class 73, the latter providing the electrical supply to the coaches. Having taken over at Edinburgh, 66737 tops a '73/9' at Aviemore with the 1S25 21.16 Euston to Inverness.

70809 powers north at Crubenmore on 25 May 2018, working the 6H51 02.48 Oxwellmains to Inverness cement train.

DRS-operated 66422 starts away from Dalwhinnie on 27 June 2019 with 4H47, the 05.04 Mossend to Inverness. An early start can be rewarding on the line around this time in the morning with the sleeper, cement and Stobart/ Tesco intermodal all to be seen.

On 25 May 2018, 43315 leads the 1S16 12.00 King's Cross to Inverness on the approach to Dalwhinnie. These services are now operated by Azuma units.

Royal train-liveried 67005 *Queen's Messenger* approaches Dalwhinnie on the morning of 25 May 2018 with 1S25, the overnight 21.16 London Euston to Inverness Caledonian Sleeper service.

43148 heads south at Drumochter on 27 June 2019 with 1B52, the 09.44 Inverness to Edinburgh. This was at a time when the stock still carried its former operator's livery of First Great Western.

The Class 170s have been the staple diet for passenger operations in Scotland for some time. With ScotRail inheriting HSTs, a number of the DMUs have found their way south of the border to operate with other train companies. As part of the process, the units have generally had their ScotRail brandings removed and therefore appear in a plain livery. 170416 is seen at Dalnacardoch on 25 May 2018 heading north with an Edinburgh to Inverness service. This particular set is now with East Midlands Railway.

Intercity Mainline-liveried 37419 makes for a colourful sight as it approaches Blair Athol on 8 August 2020 with the 1Q77 13.30 Mossend to Inverness test train. On the rear of the formation was 37402 *Stephen Middlemore 23.12.1954-8.6.2013*.

Strathclyde PTE (SPT)-liveried 320322 arrives at Anniesland on 8 July 2008 with a service for Balloch. Anniesland is the interchange point for trains to Glasgow Queen Street via Maryhill.

A Class 33 on the *Royal Scotsman*... what next! Following the award of the haulage contract to West Coast Railway Company, several unusual locos appeared on the train including Class 31s, 33s, 37s, 47s and 57s. On 18 September 2006, 33207 *Jim Martin* runs through Dalmuir while working 1H87, the 06.43 Taynuilt to Wemyss Bay. A Class 320 heads north towards Balloch on the other line.

This 1 May 2017 scene captures Colas Rail's 47739 *Robin of Templecombe* leading a North East railtour running as the 1Z71 04.41 Newcastle to Fort William on the approach to Arrochar and Tarbet.

In 2017, news broke that Colas was to run a fuel trial from Grangemouth to Fort William following the cessation of the traffic under DB. The train unfortunately ran for only a few months before the decision was made to cease operations altogether. I was fortunate enough to photograph 56302 *PECO The Railway Modeller 2016 70 Years* at Ardlui on 7 August 2017 with 6N56, the 13.31 Fort William to Grangemouth. Class 56s on the West Highland Line are certainly not common.

First ScotRail-liveried 156453 runs towards Crianlarich on 1 May 2017 with the lunchtime departure from Oban to Glasgow Queen Street. The unit will join with the service from Fort William at Crianlarich and go forward as one.

Did many people ever expect to photograph Class 73s at Oban in the 20th century? Owing to engineering works on the line from Crianlarich to Fort William, the overnight sleeper from London was diverted to Oban. Due to the lack of maintenance facilities, the train would have to run to Polmadie depot in Glasgow before returning the next day. In this most bizarre scene, 73970 is seen leaving Oban with the 5Y11 12.30 to Polmadie on 11 March 2017.

Railtours to Oban are not as common as Fort William, but when they do run, they generally use classic traction; in this instance, a pair of Class 37s courtesy of Direct Rail Services. On 12 August 2017, 37602 heads 37609 shortly after leaving Tyndrum Lower with the 1Z37 07.50 from Edinburgh Waverly as part of a 'Edinburgh Military Tattoo/Highland Fling' tour, this using the *Northern Belle* coaches.

On 18 June 2016, the 16.05 Mallaig/Fort William to Glasgow Queen Street leaves the horseshoe curve between Bridge of Orchy and Tyndrum with 156446 leading the way. The second unit would have joined 156446 at Fort William for the run south.

Every year, thousands of tourists flock to Fort William to travel behind steam locos on the line to Mallaig, crossing the famous Glenfinnan Viaduct on the 'Jacobite' train. This is operated by the West Coast Railway Company and runs twice a day; such is the popularity of the train. 45407 sets off from Fort William on 12 July 2019 with the morning train.

156493 approaches Fort William on 12 July 2019 with the first train of the day from Mallaig. The area still retains some lovely semaphore signals.

Chapter 4

Central Scotland

The scope of area that I am defining as central Scotland relates to the west end of Edinburgh through to Glasgow via Shotts, Falkirk and Bathgate along with the line as far as Perth. This is a huge region and I simply cannot cover everything; however, I have picked some interesting images that show both the variety and some of the changes that have occurred in the past 15 years.

The greatest change to these lines relates to the electrification of both the Shotts and Falkirk High routes, not to mention the lines from Glasgow to Whifflet, Cumbernauld and north to both Alloa and Dunblane. This process has seen a significant change to the rolling stock requirements. Starting out on the Shotts line, in the period I am covering, the Class 156s were the predominant power with Class 158s on occasions as time moved on. Following the completion of the wiring, the new Class 385s found themselves allocated to the services.

The main Edinburgh-Glasgow (E&G) route via Falkirk High was initially operated by Class 170s. While waiting for the Class 385s to enter service, a number of Class 365 EMUs found use on hire to cover for the delay and saw use on services between the two cities along with running between Dunblane, Alloa and Edinburgh. Within the area around Glasgow, the electrification of the line to Whifflet and Cumbernauld offered the chance to photograph EMUs such as Class 318s, 320s and 334s, not something I anticipated doing at Cumbernauld years before.

Of course, during this period, a number of new railway lines have opened including the Airdrie to Bathgate extension and the Stirling to Alloa route. These have proven to be a success and hopefully more will open in the future. On the lines heading north towards Perth, the introduction of HSTs by ScotRail has also been a popular move for the photographer.

I have included a number of images from the Bo'ness and Kinneil Railway, this preserved line deserving a mention due to the varied traction and often popular visiting locos the line attracts. The railway itself has developed somewhat in the past 15 years with a new platform now in place at Manuel, which is the end of the line where the connection to the E&G is located. Currently under construction is a second platform at Birkhill along with a signal box, which will offer a greater running opportunity than the usual one up and one down train service in place at present.

On the freight front, as before, there are simply too many workings to cover so I have selected the ones that I wanted to show and hope these provide some interest. The two focal points in this section relate to Grangemouth and Mossend, both having provided a myriad of locos and workings over the years.

Grangemouth was predominantly petroleum driven in its early years, but this has now changed and it is today a key player in the container market with both DRS and DB working trains. Fuel trains leaving this location include those to Prestwick and Dalston in Cumbria, operated by Colas. Mossend in Lanarkshire is the main marshalling point in Scotland today and is generally busy with a variety of trains, both passing and terminating. The yard also has a stabling point that Freightliner uses for its locos, these having worked trains to and from the nearby Coatbridge container terminal.

As before, coal traffic has declined in recent years, which has made a huge impact on the freight scene. Trains passing the area included those working to both Longannet Power Station on the banks of the Firth of the Forth and Cockenzie. Longannet is no longer in service while Cockenzie on the east coast of Scotland has been demolished.

Occasionally, the two ScotRail Class 68s found themselves on freight traffic, generally working the intermodal service to Aberdeen. In freezing conditions on 4 December 2016, 68006 *Daring* races north at Forteviot, between Perth and Gleneagles, with 4A13, the loaded 12.30 Grangemouth to Aberdeen.

As part of the decommissioning of the Dounreay nuclear site, DRS has been providing the motive power to move the spent waste to Sellafield. On a gorgeous 15 May 2019, 66302 and 66303 round the curve on the approach to Gleneagles with 6S99, the 05.26 Carlisle to Georgemas Junction.

BR green-liveried 37057 rounds the curve at Bardrill Road shortly after passing Blackford on 15 April 2017 working the 1Q77 13.30 Mossend to Inverness test train with 37421 on the rear. The train during this period was being operated by Colas.

Unbranded ex-First Great Western 43030 heads south at Kinbuck with an Aberdeen to Glasgow Queen Street service on 13 May 2019.

EWS liveried 66147 is seen at Kilbaggie on 12 August 2010 with the 6G07 12.28 Hunterston to Longannet loaded coal train.

Freightliner's 70004 runs through Alloa Loops on 17 September 2010 with the empty 4C07 13.26 Longannet to Ravenstruther. At times during the day, it was not uncommon to see trains passing here due to the high volume of coal Longannet required.

Shortly before the wires go live, 156508 waits to lead the 15.41 to Glasgow Queen Street at Alloa on 12 May 2018. Note the station name board in vertical format.

The SPT livery suited the Class 170s well. With the days of the livery numbered, 170478 passes Manor Powis on the Alloa line with the 14.41 Alloa to Glasgow Queen Street service on 7 June 2013.

A sight that I could never have imagined would be the use of Class 365s on Dunblane services. 365519 heads south at Cowie, between Stirling and Larbert, with a Dunblane to Edinburgh service on 2 February 2019. Note Stirling Castle in the background.

Network Rail DBSO 9701 is seen leading a test train south at Plean on 21 August 2011 with BR blue 31106 bringing up the rear. The DBSO is, of course, no stranger to this line, having seen use on the push-pull workings with the Class 47/7s years ago.

Back on 8 February 2007, 67003 passes Larbert North signal box while working the empty 5D03 Aberdeen to Motherwell parcel vans.

Ex-Wessex Alphaline-liveried 158867 works south at Larbert Junction on 17 September 2010 with a Dunblane to Glasgow Queen Street service. This was taken during a time when ScotRail had a number of units on hire, including South West Trains-liveried examples.

A location that it is no longer possible to photograph at is Greenhill Lower Junction due to the overhead wires. DB red 66101 rounds the curve on 20 April 2013 with 6A32, the 09.29 Mossend to Aberdeen. Greenhill Junction is the junction for the lines to Cumbernauld or, alternatively, Glasgow Queen Street.

Malcolm Logistics-branded 66405 is seen at Allandale on 24 May 2006 with the well-loaded 4M30 19.00 Grangemouth to Daventry intermodal.

318269, wearing the now obsolete SPT livery, enters Greenfaulds on 31 May 2014 with a Dalmuir to Cumbernauld service.

With engineering work taking place at Midcalder Junction on the line to Edinburgh from Carstairs, a number of services were diverted via Cumbernauld and Falkirk. First TransPennine Express 185131 leads a Manchester Airport to Edinburgh Waverly service north at Magiscroft on 25 May 2013.

As the storm clouds gather over Greenfaulds, 66102 leads the 6D18 16.38 Grangemouth to Mossend loaded tanks past Greenfoot on 20 April 2013. These tanks would work to Riccarton fuel terminal on the Monday morning.

Freightliner grey-liveried 86637 leads two sister locos at Coatbridge Central on 8 February 2007 with the 4M74 13.41 Coatbridge to Crewe containers.

The opening of the Airdrie to Bathgate line offered yet another route for trains to run between Glasgow and Edinburgh. On 6 April 2013, 334014 heads for Edinburgh Waverly at Hillend Loch, between Blackridge and Caldercruix.

During the electrification of the line between Carmyle and Whifflet, 66130 brings yet another loaded train of coal up from Hunterston as the 6G07 12.28 to Longannet Power Station on 10 July 2014 at Kirkwood. The train would shortly head north on the line through Cumbernauld and Larbert to reach its destination.

The demise of the ScotRail Class 314 fleet offered the chance to photograph the units being dragged south for both scrapping and component recovery, motive power being provided by Rail Operations Group Class 37s. 37884 powers upgrade towards Bailieston on 13 March 2019 towing 314204 as the 11.26 Yoker to Glasgow Works.

Following its transfer from London Midland, 320416 comes to a halt at Bargeddie on 6 August 2016 with the 09.32 Dalmuir to Whifflet service. The unit would soon be hauled to Kilmarnock for a repaint into ScotRail colours.

DRS' 66429 approaches Gartcosh on 8 October 2009 with the 4Z50 09.50 Inverness to Coatbridge containers on behalf of the Russell Group.

A regular freight flow over the Stepps line is the Alcan tanks from North Blyth to Fort William. 66736 *Wolverhampton Wanderers* is seen at Crowood Grange with the 6S45 09.25 ex-North Blyth on 14 September 2013.

On 14 September 2013, 47818 heads for Polmadie at Stepps with the 5Z31 12.52 Helensburgh to Polmadie *Northern Belle* empty coaching stock move.

With the franchise operator unconfirmed at the time the units were being built, a number of Class 170s were delivered in a variety of unbranded liveries. 170450 waits time at Glasgow Queen Street prior to forming the 11.00 to Edinburgh Waverly on 8 April 2005.

A rather colourful Network Rail test train features in the shape of 67027 in DB red with silver 67029 *Royal Diamond* on the rear as they work past Cadder Yard on 16 June 2014 with the 1Q47 10.38 Heaton to Derby via Glasgow Queen Street.

Due to delays in the introduction of the Class 385s, ScotRail hired in a number of Class 365 EMUs. On 28 June 2018, 365537 heads the 11.30 Glasgow Queen Street to Edinburgh through Greenhill Upper Junction.

The new order in Scotland are the Hitachi-built Class 385s. 385005 leads the 14.15 Edinburgh Waverly to Glasgow through Greenhill Upper on 29 August 2018.

EWS-liveried 66041 leads a string of HAA hoppers through Falkirk Grahamston on 1 June 2007 with a loaded Hunterston to Longannet coal train. Note the blue band on the first wagon, which was a trademark sign that the wagon had received maintenance at Ayr Depot.

The launch of the Stobart/Tesco intermodal train from Daventry to Grangemouth saw DRS brand one of its locos in Stobart colours, 66411 also gaining the name *Eddie the Engine*. On 30 May 2007, the loco is seen getting underway from Grangemouth with the 4M48 17.40 to Daventry.

Colas' 60095 comes to a halt at Fouldubbs on the Grangemouth freight-only branch with the 6M34 19.05 to Dalston loaded tanks on 17 July 2017. The train at the time was running earlier than normal due to the ongoing electrification works in the area.

Looking resplendent on a beautiful 29 September 2013, 20309 and 20308 race past Lathallan with the 1Z23 11.45 Dalmuir to Pitlochry railtour.

This 2017 image shows the change that electrification brought at Lathallan, near Polmont, as 66558 makes for an unusual sight as it works the diverted 4M49 Coatbridge to Daventry intermodal on 17 April 2017.

To promote the opening of the Borders Railway line from Edinburgh, ScotRail branded 170414 into a promotional livery. On 26 April 2015, the unit is seen racing along the E&G at Whitecross leading the 16.00 Edinburgh Waverly to Glasgow Queen Street service.

A photo that would be impossible to replicate today for a number of reasons is that at Whitecross. Overhead wires are in situ, Virgin no longer runs the West Coast franchise, 37175 *W S Sellar* is no longer with the Scottish Railway Preservation Society (SRPS) and a new platform has been built for trains coming up from Bo'ness. 221107 leads the diverted 1M60 15.57 Edinburgh to Carlisle while 37175 runs round the 15.35 from Bo'ness on 6 April 2013.

The station at Bo'ness provides a lot of interest with the diesel depot and museum an option to visit between trains. 27001 awaits departure on 14 October 2018 with the 15.35 to Manuel.

Super power at the 2015 diesel gala in the shape of 50017 *Royal Oak* carrying the Network SouthEast livery. On 25 July 2015, the loco is seen shortly after leaving Bo'ness with the 11.30 Bo'ness to Manuel service.

62712 *Morayshire* is seen soon after departure from Bo'ness on 24 October 2015 with a Bo'ness to Manuel service during the annual steam gala.

In this image, the Class 303 appears to be running under its own power with the propelling Class 27 just out of sight round the curve. 303032 approaches Kinneil Halt with a service for Manuel on 29 July 2012.

Furness *No. 20* makes for an unique sight on 24 October 2015 as it approaches Kinneil with an afternoon service for Birkhill. The train on this occasion is using the line's two Caledonian coaches.

Hired in from West Coast Railways, 47854 rounds the curve on the approach to Snab Bridge with the 12.00 Bo'ness to Birkhill on 28 September 2008.

BR green-liveried 40106 *Atlantic Conveyor* applies the power as it starts the climb from Snab Bridge uphill to Birkhill on 25 July 2015 with the 09.30 from Bo'ness to Manuel.

This scene at Birkhill has now changed with a new platform and signal box under construction. In this shot taken on 1 June 2014, the line's sole-surviving Class 126 DMU waits to return to Bo'ness.

Once a month, Network Rail's New Measurement Train HST runs to Glasgow Queen Street. 43062 *John Armitt* leads the 1Q24 10.37 Heaton to Heaton past Park Farm, east of Linlithgow, on 17 July 2017.

Between operating the Fife loco-hauled services when under DB control, the stock was taken to Perth for cleaning, which offered the chance to record the train on the Edinburgh to Glasgow line east of Polmont. On 8 September 2010, 67021 passes Linlithgow with the 5B24 13.29 Perth to Millerhill stock move.

The *Royal Scotsman* often stabled at Bo'ness where light maintenance was carried out between duties. On 25 May 2013, 47237 storms through Philpstoun with the 5H79 12.12 empty stock for Edinburgh Waverly.

The impressive Almond Viaduct near Edinburgh rarely features in print. On a day when engineering work was taking place at Midcalder Junction, GBRf had to divert the 6S45 09.25 Blyth to Fort William Alcan tanks via Falkirk. 66737 *Lesia* leads the train on 25 May 2013.

170458 is seen pausing at Edinburgh Park, which was opened in 2003, with a Bathgate to Edinburgh Waverly service on 23 November 2007.

On its booked route, 66733 *Cambridge PSB* passes the station at Breich with the 6S45 09.25 Blyth to Fort William on 24 February 2018. In the background, electrification work is in progress with mast erection underway. Breich received quite an impressive upgrade following the work.

On a gorgeous morning when I was able to photograph two Class 47 workings in the space of an hour, 47843 *Vulcan* races along the straight towards Breich on 8 August 2015 while working the 1Z67 06.46 GB Railfreight tour from Glasgow to Scarborough.

First Group-liveried 156450 is seen between Fauldhouse and Breich on 20 July 2013 as it works an express service from Edinburgh Waverly to Glasgow Central.

After GBRf took over the haulage of the Caledonian Sleeper services, it hired in Riviera Class 47s for a number of diversions over the Shotts line. On 23 May 2015, 47812 passes Hartwood with the 5B26 08.30 Edinburgh Waverly to Polmadie empty sleeper stock.

Chapter 5
The South West

This section of the book also covers a fairly large geographical area that takes in the West Coast Main Line north from Carlisle to Glasgow, the various lines in and around the west side of the city and down the coast to both Ayr and Stranraer, along with the former Glasgow and South Western line via Kilmarnock and Dumfries.

Following the demise of loco-hauled services by Virgin, all express services in the period of this book were operated either by Class 220/221 Voyager or Class 390 Pendolino units, which took away a little of the interest of the main passenger services. While not particularly exciting to the photographer, the units transformed the workings for the better between Glasgow and London, along with services further afield to the West of England. Fortunately, a few unique liveries have appeared over the years, some of which are included. During December 2019, Virgin lost the franchise and it is now operated by Avanti, with a welcome change of livery.

A new name appeared on the West Coast Main Line during the review period in the shape of TransPennine Express. These trains ran predominantly from Manchester Airport to both Edinburgh and Glasgow. In the beginning, Class 185s were used, these then giving way to Class 350s and, more recently, Class 397s, which are in service today.

Moving into the Glasgow area, passenger services for ScotRail were in the hands of a variety of EMU types, including the Class 314s, which have recently been withdrawn from service. During the period, the Class 380s and Class 385s have come on stream and settled into service, although the latter is more common operating out of Glasgow Queen Street rather than Central. Amongst the DMUs, little has changed with Class 156s the most prominent type to be seen working all East Kilbride, Kilmarnock, Carlisle and Stranraer services.

As the railway has continued to develop, a number of lines have been electrified including the Paisley Canal branch. A third track was laid between Shields Junction and Paisley to increase the capacity of the lines heading towards Ayr, and a new line was opened to Larkhall, near Motherwell. Glasgow Central has also seen development with what was formerly the car park now rebuilt into two platforms; such is the growth in passenger numbers in recent times.

Freight on the West Coast Main Line has provided a huge amount of variety over the past 15 years, with coal, intermodal/freightliner traffic, mixed freights, tank and nuclear trains to mention just a few. Likewise, the loco variety has offered many interesting photo opportunities with older locos such as the Class 86s blending into the scene, along with the modern designs of the Class 68s and 88s. The majority of the workings that travel over the West Coast Main Line are generally bound for Mossend, Coatbridge or Grangemouth.

There has been a significant decline in coal traffic over the period. On the west coast, Hunterston was responsible for trainloads to both Longannet and Cockenzie, along with many services heading south over the border into England. This facility has now been demolished and is unlikely to see any coal services again.

Further down the coast at Ayr, Falkland Yard was the hub in the west of Scotland for coal traffic with many trains using the yard to either stable or recess. However, Falkland Yard is now steadily becoming a jungle of empty and overgrown tracks while the nearby Ayr loco maintenance depot has been demolished. Other locations that were rail served included the branches to Riccarton and Deanside, both of these no longer seeing any freight traffic. The area is simply too large for me to cover everything, but I have picked a variety of classes and liveries to show some of the workings I have photographed over the period.

Class 91s on the West Coast Main Line are unheard of apart from in recent years when East Coast services were diverted via Carlisle and the Tyne Valley line due to engineering work. 91122 races south on 29 September 2018 with 1E06, the 15.38 Edinburgh Waverly to London King's Cross service, at Springfield, north of Gretna.

On the basis that only three Freightliner Class 86/6s received the Powerhaul livery, I was rather pleased to find a pair working south at Bodsbury on 25 September 2015 with 4M74, the 13.41 Coatbridge to Crewe Basford Hall, with 86622 leading the way.

Freightliner's 66616 climbs towards Beattock at Bodsbury on 28 September 2011 with a loaded 6E31 09.28 Ravenstruther to Drax Power Station.

The latest addition to the freight scene in Scotland has been the Class 88s, which work for Direct Rail Services. The type has been relatively trouble free and settled down on the company's container traffic. 88010 *Aurora* passes Crawford on 29 November 2017 with the daily 4S43 06.16 Daventry to Mossend Stobart Tesco train.

TransPennine Express unit 185116 races south at Crawford on 25 August 2018 with the 1M98 13.09 Glasgow Central to Manchester Airport. The unit is carrying promotional 'Bee in the city' advertisements to encourage people to visit Manchester and its various attractions.

A neat little train in the shape of inspection saloon 975025 *Caroline* with 37419 *Carl Haviland 1954-2012* providing the power heads south at Castle Hill, between Abington and Crawford, on 14 July 2016 with a 5Z02 14.34 Dalmuir to Carlisle empty stock move.

390006 wearing what was to become the final version of the Virgin Trains livery on the West Coast Main Line is seen heading south at Abington loops on 25 August 2018.

First ScotRail-liveried 90024 works south at Abington on 23 June 2015 while leading the well-loaded 4M25 06.05 Mossend to Daventry intermodal.

Adorned with a special rainbow vinyl and named *Virgin Pride*, 390045 works the 9M60 16.52 Edinburgh Waverly to London Euston south at Abington on 19 April 2019.

As the first frost of the winter sets in, First TransPennine Express Desiro 350407 heads south at Wandel Mill, between Lamington and Abington, with a morning service from Edinburgh Waverly to Manchester Airport on 25 November 2016.

A rather scruffy West Coast Railways' 47245 works south past Wandel Mill on 30 September 2013 with the 5Z47 06.30 Bo'ness to Carnforth empty coaching stock move.

Every now and again, photographers find themselves in the right place at the right time and, even more unusually, in good weather. On the morning of 23 June 2015, I had been photographing in the Clyde Valley at Wandel Mill when 67026 *Diamond Jubilee* appeared heading the Royal train north to Edinburgh.

The DRS-liveried pair of 57007 and 57003 heads south at Wandel Mill on 16 August 2012 with 6M50, the 15.12 Torness to Carlisle nuclear flask train.

A diverted east coast service, running as the 1E17 13.23 Edinburgh to King's Cross, heads south at Wandel Mill on 1 October 2016 with hired-in East Midlands power car 43081 leading the way. The train would head over the Tyne Valley line to Newcastle at Carlisle.

2019 appears to have been the final full year for the ageing Freightliner Class 86 fleet, with additional Class 90s acquired from Anglia Railways likely to replace them. In glorious lighting on 28 June 2019, 86605 leads the 4M11 18.15 Coatbridge to Crewe freightliner through Lamington.

70013 *Oliver Cromwell* applies the power away from Carstairs South Junction on 24 March 2012 with the 1Z34 13.46 Edinburgh to Manchester Victoria railtour.

Alstom-branded 390004 heads away from Carstairs on 21 October 2012 with a Glasgow Central to London Euston service.

Freightliner Class 70s looked purposeful on coal trains, which they were used on to a variety of locations including Longannet, Hunterston and a number of the loading sites in Ayrshire. On 27 April 2011, 70005 approaches Carstairs on the West Coast Main Line with the empty 4S42 09.50 Fiddlers Ferry to Hunterston.

An early start is required to record the overnight sleeper from London Euston to Glasgow and Edinburgh. Shortly before the contract to supply locos went over to GB Railfreight, EWS-liveried 90026 waits at Carstairs with the 1B26 06.30 to Edinburgh Waverly on 26 July 2014. Carstairs is the station where the portions for Edinburgh and Glasgow join and split.

Class 91s ran through to Glasgow Central with a number of services from London King's Cross. In a transitional combination of liveries, East Coast's 91106 passes Ravenstruther on 27 April 2011 with a service for Glasgow.

GBRf-liveried 92032 *IMechE Railway Division* heads north at Ravenstruther on 21 April 2014 with a well loaded 6S51 12.55 Carlisle Yard to Mossend, this conveying Network Rail autoballaster wagons.

Occasionally, the mail workings from Shieldmuir require loco haulage owing to issues with the Class 325s. On 10 February 2006, it was the turn of DRS' 47802 to tow the 1M44 15.31 Shieldmuir to Warrington mail train. Seen approaching Cleghorn level crossing, near Lanark, former DRS stablemate 87006 was coupled behind.

Carmine and cream-liveried 318253 passes Cleghorn level crossing with a morning Lanark to Milngavie service on 10 February 2006.

Stobart-liveried *92017 Bart the Engine* was on the correct train on 27 April 2011 as it headed north at Craigenhill with the daily 4S43 06.16 Daventry to Mossend Tesco train.

Back in 2007, the Class 334s were regular visitors to Lanark. 334039 approaches Carluke on 15 August 2007 with a Milngavie to Lanark service.

The EWS pairing of 37422 *Cardiff Canton* and 37417 *Richard Trevithick* rumbles through Uddingston with the 1Z30 15.27 Glasgow Central to Crewe railtour on 25 August 2008. This tour had taken in the Alloa line and Deanside branch earlier in the day.

Prior to the Colas invasion, all cement workings in Scotland were managed by Freightliner. 66618 *Railways Illustrated Annual Photographic Awards Alan Barnes* powers past Rutherglen on 15 August 2007 with 6D62, the loaded 07.52 Oxwellmains to Viewpark, this being formed of PCA tanks.

The Class 314s bowed out of service for ScotRail during 2019. Back in happier times on 11 July 2009, 314215 approaches Burnside with a Glasgow Central to Newton service.

'Skinhead' 31106 rests at Glasgow Central platform 1 on 1 March 2011 while working a 2Q88 Craigentinny to Mossend track recording test train.

314202 was one of the last Class 314s to retain the Strathclyde PTE orange and black livery. On 8 August 2006, the unit is seen at Glasgow Central with an early morning service for the Cathcart circle.

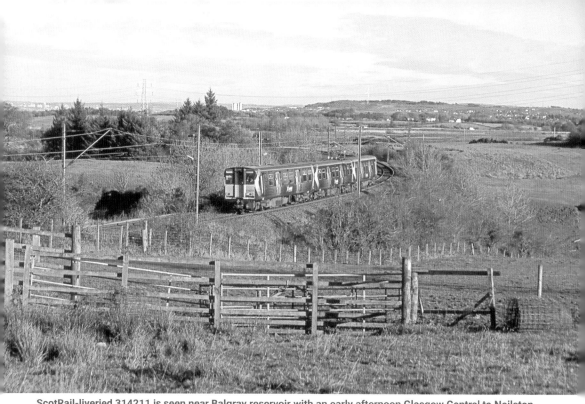

ScotRail-liveried 314211 is seen near Balgray reservoir with an early afternoon Glasgow Central to Neilston service on 27 October 2018.

On 13 July 2005, Pathfinder Tours ran the 'Celtic Freighter' railtour to a number of freight-only lines in the west of Scotland. At the start of their journey to Ayrshire, 37029 and 37229 shatter the peace at Crossmyloof in the Glasgow suburbs with the 1Z60 Glasgow Central to Birmingham International via Riccarton and Knockshinnoch.

Riccarton fuel terminal in Kilmarnock no longer receives any rail traffic following a decline in its requirements. Shortly before the contract came to an end, 70802 passes Priesthill and Darnley with 6D61, the empty 12.48 from Riccarton to Grangemouth, on 19 June 2017.

66428 rumbles through Hillington West on 9 March 2011 with the 4N78 12.56 Elderslie to Grangemouth intermodal. This was taken prior to the Paisley corridor project, which provided a third track to increase capacity on this section of line.

Juniper 334004 arrives into Paisley St James station with a Gourock to Glasgow Central service on 2 November 2010.

380115 lays over at Largs on 18 April 2015 prior to forming a service to Glasgow Central. The Class 380s took over all the workings out of Glasgow down to Ayr and Largs and have proved incredibly reliable.

The days of DRS Class 37s on nuclear trains looks to be over. However, back on 8 April 2015, 37602 and 37667 were in charge of 6M22, the 12.30 Hunterston to Sellafield, as they pass Stevenston.

With a storm brewing over Irvine, 66559 heads south at Gailles with a loaded Hunterston to Fiddlers Ferry coal train on 31 March 2015.

Tornado at Troon! I made a concerted effort to drive to Troon on 27 June 2015 to photograph 60163 heading the 1Z51 10.08 Carlisle to Carlisle tour titled 'The Borders Reivers'. It is not that often that steam-hauled trains run over the Ayr line and I wanted to record it somewhere recognisable.

Petroleum sector liveried 60054 *Charles Babbage* heads north at Lochgreen on 26 January 2009 with the empty 6N44 14.30 Prestwick Airport to Grangemouth tanks.

Freightliner Heavy Haul coal workings were plentiful in 2010 in the south west of Scotland. 66559 passes my home station of Prestwick Town on 20 August 2010 with the empty 4S28 13.12 Carlisle to Killoch Colliery.

For a long time, EWS/DB worked the Prestwick aviation fuel train using a Class 66. The train at the time would work from Grangemouth to Prestwick via a run-round at Falkland Yard, which was required on the basis that the airport siding is north facing. On a warm 28 June 2011, 66096 heads through Prestwick with the loaded 6R46 06.32 ex-Grangemouth.

A rather bleak looking Falkland Yard following the demise of coal traffic now offers an opportunity to photograph trains entering from the north. Previously, the sidings in the foreground were full of coal wagons. 56302 *PECO The Railway Modeller 2016 70 Years* slows down as it enters the loop on 26 September 2017 while working the loaded 6R46 06.32 Grangemouth to Prestwick Airport aviation fuel train.

For a number of years, Freightliner worked loaded cement trains to Ayr Harbour for export to Ireland. 66606 catches the last of the evening sunshine on 16 October 2006 as it eases out of Falkland Yard while working the return 6Z65 16.21 Ayr Harbour to Oxwellmains.

Ayr station features in this photo of 31465 heading south with a combined Network Rail ultrasonic and structure gauging test train, which was running as the 3Q15 15.38 Falkland Yard to Mossend on 12 April 2011.

156432 pulls away from Maybole on 9 June 2007 while working an Ayr to Girvan service.

The hills south of Girvan at Pinmore are reverberating to the sound of 37607 as it heads south with the 'Galloway Galloper' railtour, this running as the 1Z94 06.27 Glasgow Central to Stranraer. This tour took in a number of freight-only lines, including those at Killoch and Chalmerston. The photograph was taken on 12 February 2011.

Steam-hauled trains on the Stranraer line have always proven popular with some challenging stretches of track for the locos to tackle. On a day when the weather was quite simply awful, 44871 leads the 'Great Britain' railtour south at New Luce with the 1Z25 08.39 Edinburgh to Stranraer, this being one of the few sunny spells on 30 April 2014.

Colas Rail's 47749 *City of Truro* passes Crosshouse, between Kilmarnock and Barassie, on 10 August 2017 while working 5Z73, the 09.49 Polmadie to Kilmarnock (Brodie Rail), this conveying Mk3a sleeper coach 10605 for maintenance.

During a refurbishment programme for the Class 334s, Virgin Class 57s were initially used to move the units to and from Kilmarnock. On 2 May 2012, 57307 *Lady Penelope* sets back at Kilmarnock station into the Brodie workshops with the 6Z52 09.28 Glasgow Works to Kilmarnock, this conveying the brake force tanks and barrier coaches necessary to move the units.

By August 2013, the Class 334 drags were being hauled by 55022 *Royal Scots Grey*. On 17 August 2013, the loco is seen pulling a refurbished 334015 out of the works at Kilmarnock with the 6Z54 to Yoker depot.

Class 60s have long had an association with the long-haul coal trains from Scotland. By 2005, their use was diminishing as Class 66s took over the majority of workings. On 17 October 2005, 60071 *Ribblehead Viaduct* was unusually allocated to the 6M32 11.38 Falkland Yard-Bescot. The train is seen at the single line token point at Blackhouse Junction, heading for Mauchline.

EWS-liveried 66058 climbs out of Mossblown on 21 February 2015 with a loaded Hunterston to Carlisle Yard coal train. Demand for coal was still high enough at this time to warrant Saturday workings.

Aggregate Industries-liveried 66711 eases onto the Enterkine Viaduct and across the River Ayr on 29 September 2017 with an early running 6E02 19.00 Killoch Colliery to Drax Power Station loaded coal train. The large number of speed restrictions on this branch allowed for an easy drive to get several photos of the same train.

For a number of years, it was perfectly common to see the use of diesel drags over the Glasgow South Western line due to engineering work on the West Coast Main Line north of Carlisle. In late evening sunshine, 57303 *Alan Tracy* rounds the curve at Polquhap, between Cumnock and New Cumnock, with the 1M19 16.05 Glasgow Central to Euston on 14 April 2006. The Class 57 would be removed from the Pendolino at Carlisle.

66747 was one of three Class 66s brought to the UK by GBRf from Holland. Still retaining its previous owner's livery, the loco is almost at the top of the climb to Polquhap Summit on 16 April 2015 with the loaded 6H97 15.00 Greenburn to Drax Power Station. The train will travel north to Kilmarnock to run round before retracing its steps past the same location in two hours' time heading to Carlisle.

One of the most enjoyable things I have done as a photographer in the south west of Scotland was recording the Ayrshire coal scene and its variety of branches. The Greenburn opencast site near New Cumnock was responsible for up to three trains a day at one point, most destined for Drax Power Station. In this charming scene on 17 May 2017, 66701 approaches Boig crossing with 4S66, the 06.49 empties from Tyne Dock.

What was to become the last train in Scotland to operate with HAA wagons was a Warrington to New Cumnock. On 17 July 2008, 66204 sets back into Crowbandsgate with the empty 6S13 06.38 ex-Warrington. The loading point here involved a pad with mechanical shovels loading the train.

A mixed pairing of Class 156 liveries features in this photo of 156512 and a sister unit heading north at New Cumnock on 11 April 2009 with a Carlisle to Glasgow Central service.

DB red-liveried 66118 looks superb at the head of the 6K14 11.40 Beattock to Carlisle Yard infrastructure working on 31 May 2020 as it passes Closeburn, north of Dumfries.

Further reading from

As Europe's leading transport publisher, we produce a wide range of market-leading railway magazines.